# the official
# celtic
# annual

# 2001

**Written by**
**Douglas Russell**

# g

A Grange Publication

© 2000. Published by Grange Communications Ltd., Edinburgh, under licence from Celtic Football Club.
Printed in the EU.

ISBN 1 902704 05 3

£5.99

# contents

# THE MAN IN C

## PLAYING CAREER

1971: Leaves Distillery in October of this year and signs for Nottingham Forest. Also makes his international debut (as substitute) when Northern Ireland play USSR.

1978: It's 'double' celebrations as Forest win both the League Championship and League Cup.

1979: Collects his second League Cup medal as Forest retain the trophy after their 3-2 final triumph over Southampton.

1980: Overseas success quickly follows when Hamburg are beaten 1-0 in the European Cup Final in Madrid.

1981: Transfers to Norwich after some 285 appearances and 48 goals.

With just 11 outings (and 1 goal) in his new colours, Martin is on the move again - this time to Manchester City.

1982: Returns to Norwich in January of this year having only played a dozen or so games with the Maine Road club. Makes some 54 appearances and nets 11 goals.

1983: Joins Notts County in August where he will score 5 times in over 60 outings.

1984: Awarded international cap number 64 (his last) when Northern Ireland defeat Finland 2-1.

## MANAGERIAL CAREER

1990: Appointed manager of non-league side Wycombe Wanderers.

1991: Win the FA Trophy.

1993: Repeats the trophy success but, more importantly, takes the GM Vauxhall Conference title and promotion to the Football League.

1994: Wycombe are then promoted from Division 3 at their first attempt.

1995: After a short stay as manager of Norwich, Martin accepts an offer to fill the same role at Leicester.

1996: Crystal Palace are beaten 2-1 in the play-off finals and Leicester are promoted to the Premiership.

1997: Takes Leicester into Europe for the first time in 35 years following their defeat of Middlesbrough in the Coca-Cola Cup final. His team finish a very credible ninth in the Premiership that season.

1998 : Leicester finish tenth in the Championship.

1999 : Spurs (with a last-minute goal) deny his side another trophy when the Londoners take the Worthington Cup.

2000 : Tranmere are beaten 2-1 at Wembley as Martin's side lift the Worthington Cup. Leicester finish eighth in the Premiership (their highest-ever placing) and thus qualify for the UEFA Cup tournament of Season 2000/2001.

HARGE

# HAIL C

**BILLY McNEILL - A CELTIC LEGEND**   *mcneill!*

It is difficult to imagine a more appropriate nickname for such a great figure in Celtic history as Billy McNeill, who served the club so magnificently as player, captain and manager. As the lynchpin of the defence and overall inspiration, Billy was the pivotal figure of the legendary Jock Stein squads of the 1960s and early 1970s.

As well as holding the line at the heart of the defence, 'Caesar' regularly ventured forward for set-pieces and corners. This habit produced three of the most memorable moments of not only Billy's but Celtic's history of that time.

The whole glorious Jock Stein era really began with the 1965 Scottish Cup Final victory over Dunfermline, in which McNeill headed the dramatic winner. Similarly, but perhaps more importantly, the great captain stepped up to steer home the most sensational of last-gasp winners (with just seconds to spare) in the European Cup quarter-final at Celtic Park against Vojvodina Novi Sad of Yugoslavia in Season 1966/67. The third 'wonder' goal was the first-minute opener in the crushing 4-0 Scottish Cup Final win over Rangers in 1969.

# AESAR!

Perhaps, however, the defining image of a glorious career (9 League Championships, 7 Scottish Cups, 6 League Cups and 1 European Cup) was, in fact, its very pinnacle as Billy hoisted the massive European Cup aloft in that unforgettable pose which flashed around the world to acclaim the majestic new kings of Europe.

As manager of the club, it was Billy McNeill who, amongst other triumphs, masterminded the breathtaking 'Centenary Double' of Season 1987/88.

Hail, Caesar! A true Celtic 'great' if ever there was one.

# THE FUTURE'S GREEN

## YOUNG GUNS AND A NEW BEGINNING

The record books confirm that Celtic's last league game of Season 1999/2000 resulted in a 2-0 home victory over tangerine rivals from the City of Discovery, Dundee United. Some neutrals would, no doubt, suggest that this was nothing but a meaningless end of season game with little or nothing at stake. Fair enough comment, many would agree. But, in truth, there was much more to it than that and, in many ways, this game was about the future well-being of Celtic Football Club.

The 'Bhoys' starting line-up that day included, quite amazingly, no fewer than six youngsters, all under the age of twenty. Brian McColligan, Jim Goodwin and Ryan McCann (all making their first-team debut) appeared alongside John Kennedy, Mark Fotheringham and Simon Lynch, talented son of the defender who netted the penalty winner in the Scottish Cup Final triumph over Rangers in 1977.

Fittingly, it was Simon Lynch (giving a quite superb performance on the day) who claimed Celtic's first, in the second period of play, with a blistering shot high into the net following Mjallby's cut-back into a crowded penalty area. Finishing of the highest order! Indeed, the youngster might have scored a 'hat-trick' but two subsequent efforts only bulged the side netting of 'keeper Alan Combe's goal. The young 'Bhoy' did, however, earn his side a penalty but Eyal Berkovic failed to capitalise from the subsequent spot-kick.

It was one of the day's three debutants who made Celtic's second. Mark Burchill duly converted following good work by Ryan McCann after he had charged through the United defence and shot for goal.

Although, understandably, the longest and loudest cheers of the day were reserved for substitute and returning hero Henrik Larrson (back, sooner than anticipated, after that Lyon nightmare), the Celtic faithful also recognised the significance of the part played – and, hopefully, to be played in years to come – by a group of youngsters with their future very much in front of them.

And that future is, of course, a particular shade of green.

# BUSINESS

larsson larsson larsson larsson larsson larsson larsson larsson

*Scotland and Europe be warned. The 'Bhoy' is back . . . and he means business!*

# AS USUAL

## HENRIK LARSSON

Celtic's defeat, by a solitary goal, in the UEFA Cup tie of October 1999, was nothing compared to their other loss that black night in the French city of Lyon. The horrendous leg injury suffered by Henrik Larsson (the club's most influential player?) was seen by many neutrals as the defining moment of the 'Bhoys' season. A particularly cruel blow to those who live and breath Celtic considering how well the Swede and, indeed, the team had been playing prior to this tragedy. (It is worth noting that, after winning their next Premier League encounter with St. Johnstone three days later, Celtic had made their best start to a season since 1974/75).

Henrik, himself, had started the league campaign in quite scintillating form, scoring two in Celtic's crushing 5-0 defeat of Aberdeen at Pittodrie on the first day of August. Further strikes followed in quick succession against Cwmbran Town (a 'double' in the EUFA Cup, 12.8.99), Dundee (his last minute winner secured a 2-1 victory, 21.8.99), Hearts (4-0, 29.8.99) and Tel Aviv (another 'double' in the EUFA Cup, 16.9.99). By the time that he had claimed a marvellous 'hat-trick' in the 7-0 'home' annihilation of Aberdeen in mid October, Celtic had played thirteen competitive matches with statistics showing a total of forty-two goals scored and only three conceded. Needless to say, confidence was high as the 'Bhoys' headed for France on European business shortly after that Aberdeen encounter.

Instead of dwelling on a cruel, dark October night far from home, let us fast forward to the sunshine of Saturday 20th May, 2000 (and Celtic's last game of the league campaign) when over 47,500 people rose as one to salute the return of one of their favourite sons. With some 65 minutes on the clock, substitute Henrik Larsson took to the field with a cheer ringing in his ears that could be heard, no doubt, by supporters of a certain other team on the south-west side of Glasgow. It was certainly some welcome but, then again, he's certainly some player.

This was not Larsson's last game of the season, however, as the player made it to EURO 2000 as part of the Swedish squad. In fact, in the eyes of many, he netted one of the goals of the championship in his country's third, section game when Italy were the opponents. Sweden's equaliser, it was superbly finished-off, after a 'one-on-one' with Francesco Toldo - probably the best goalkeeper on view in the low countries last summer. Henrik Larsson had made his mark in, what was to become, one of the great football tournaments.

HENRIK IS BACK!

larsson larsson larsson

WINNERS

# WHO WON WHAT

THE MANAGERS' RECORD

WILLIE MALEY (1897-1940)
16 LEAGUE CHAMPIONSHIPS, 14 SCOTTISH CUPS PLUS
GLASGOW EXHIBITION TROPHY (1902) AND
EMPIRE EXHIBITION TROPHY (1938)

JIMMY MCSTAY (1940-1945)
VICTORY IN EUROPE CUP (1945)

JIMMY MCGRORY (1945-1965)
1 LEAGUE CHAMPIONSHIP, 2 SCOTTISH CUPS, 2 LEAGUE
CUPS PLUS ST. MUNGO CUP (1951) AND
CORONATION CUP (1953)

JOCK STEIN (1965-1978)
10 LEAGUE CHAMPIONSHIPS, 8 SCOTTISH CUPS,
6 LEAGUE CUPS AND 1 EUROPEAN CUP (1967)

BILLY MCNEILL (1978-1983)
3 LEAGUE CHAMPIONSHIPS, 1 SCOTTISH CUP AND
1 LEAGUE CUP

DAVID HAY (1983-1987)
1 LEAGUE CHAMPIONSHIP AND 1 SCOTTISH CUP

BILLY MCNEILL (1987-1991)
1 LEAGUE CHAMPIONSHIP AND 2 SCOTTISH CUPS

LIAM BRADY (1991-1993)

LOU MACARI (1993-1994)

TOMMY BURNS (1994-1997)
1 SCOTTISH CUP

WIM JANSEN (1997-1998)
1 LEAGUE CHAMPIONSHIP AND 1 LEAGUE CUP

JOSEF VENGLOS (1998-1999)

JOHN BARNES (1999-2000)

KENNY DALGLISH (INTERIM HEAD COACH 2000)
1 LEAGUE CUP

# A SILVER SUND

## CIS Insurance Cup I

### Aberdeel
### Riseth (14 minutes),

There can be no doubt that Aberdeen approached this game with more than just a little apprehension. After all, Celtic had blasted an amazing 18 goals past the team from the granite city, without reply, in their three previous (league) encounters - with scores of 5-0, 7-0 and 6-0 respectively. Naturally, the bets were all on Celts to lift this trophy with many Aberdeen fans travelling to the national stadium probably more in hope than anything else. Certainly, few neutrals would be anticipating 'red' celebrations at the end of the ninety minutes. Although only(!) two goals eventually separated the teams, it was, nonetheless, a quite emphatic victory that the 'green and whites' celebrated long and hard into the night.

Celtic started well and struck after only fourteen minutes - from a rather unlikely and surprising source. Following a throw-in deep in Aberdeen territory, Moravcik fed Wieghorst. The Dane's subsequent ball across the penalty area was met by the left foot of Vidar Riseth who unceremoniously beat the diving Jim Leighton from close range. The 'Hoops' were one-up. Although that was the only goal of the first forty-five minutes, Celtic had dominated proceedings with both Wieghorst and Petrov controlling the midfield zone to great effect, cancelling-out their opposite numbers, and Jonathan Gould a virtual spectator.

Early in the second-half with 58 minutes on the clock, the lead was doubled. Moravcik found Viduka who then slipped the ball wide to Tommy Johnson. The striker made no mistake as he drove the ball into the corner of the net, with Leighton again well beaten. That, as they say, was that and it was all over bar the shouting. Certainly Celtic could (and indeed should) have scored more, especially in the last ten minutes when Aberdeen miraculously survived four close encounters of the green kind.

CHAM
CHAI
CHAM
CHAM

88

# AY IN THE PARK

**nal, 19 March 2000.**

**Celtic 2**

**hnson (58 minutes)**

First, and most spectacular, of the quartet was an audacious 30 yard lob by the artist known as Lubo which struck the crossbar with Leighton scrambling back after being caught in no man's land. The 'keeper then saved well from Wieghorst before both Viduka and Jackie McNamara had efforts cleared off the line by defenders McAllister and Perry in turn.

Although it had been a real team effort from defence to attack, many fans felt that Tommy Johnson deserved particular praise considering the misfortune with injury that the player had endured since arriving in Glasgow some three years earlier. No-one celebrated more than him during the traditional lap of honour ... and all the time, the huge Celtic support sang the afternoon away!

Celtic : Gould, Riseth, Mjallby, Boyd, Mahe, McNamara, Petrov, Wieghorst, Moravcik, Viduka and Johnson.
Subs : Kerr, Stubbs, Berkovic.

The Road to Hampden :
Third Round
Ayr 0, Celtic 4(Viduka, Blinker, Mjallby, Petta)

Fourth Round
Celtic 1(Wieghorst), Dundee 0

Semi-final
Celtic 1 (Moravcik), Kilmarnock 0

PIONS
PIONS
PIONS
PIONS

# KING OF COOL

## A LOOK BACK TO A MEMORABLE DAY IN THE CAREER OF JOHN COLLINS, A CELTIC GREAT

The 'Old Firm' encounter of 30th April, 1994, at Ibrox was even more unique than usual as the 46,000 fans gathered inside the stadium were (officially) all Rangers supporters!  Followers of the 'Hoops' had not been allowed to purchase tickets for this league game (although some, hardly surprisingly, did manage to attend events in Govan that day 'in silence') which ensured that the atmosphere, to say the least, was somewhat unreal.  Keeping cool heads in this intimidating arena would not be a problem for the visitors, however, as the Celtic captain that day was none other than John Collins - the iceman himself.

After a torrid opening, during which the inevitable onslaught from the home side was brilliantly contained, that 'man of ice' image was underlined when Collins superbly netted the opener.  With some twenty-nine minutes on the clock, he calmly bent a free-kick (from just outside the penalty area) over the defensive wall into the tightest corner of Rangers' goal.  As the ball curled unstoppably into the right hand corner past the despairing, outstretched hand of 'keeper Scott, two classic pop tracks of the 1960s-'Sound of Silence' and 'A Kind of Hush'-sprang to mind.  The stunned crowd reaction (or non-reaction) was quite unreal.  Had Collins not read the script?

No one should have been in the least surprised though, for this was, in fact, the player's fourth goal in the previous five 'Old Firm' derbies.  An impressive strike rate, in anyone's book, by a masterly midfielder who always led by example.  His, and Celtic's, opening strike in the 2-1 Ibrox premier league triumph of October 1993 had been just as stunning.

On the day of this infamous Ibrox lock-out, the player had once again inspired his men to a level of commitment which came so close to turning the threatened nightmare into a dream that eerie afternoon in Govan.  Even although the game ended in a 1-1 draw (Rangers equalised with a 'deflected' goal in the second-half), this 'moral victory' tasted so, so sweet.

And at the centre of it all was John Collins.  Without doubt, one of the 'coolest' men ever to wear the green of Celtic.

# BURNS' BHOYS

**Premier League, 27th August, 1994**
**RANGERS 0  CELTIC 2**
**Collins (45 mins), McStay (47 mins)**

Some games remain engraved in the mind for a long time, others simply fade away almost before the final whistle has blown and the fans begin to disperse with thoughts only of that night's dinner.  Few Celtic fans, however, would have forgotten this warm afternoon at Ibrox Stadium in the early days of Season 1994/95.

New manager Tommy Burns left Govan that Saturday p.m. walking on air, having witnessed his side's virtual destruction of Rangers in a breathtaking display of attacking football, laced with classic Celtic skill and flair aplenty.

Virtually from the start, John Collins, Paul McStay and Pat McGinlay exerted a stranglehold in the centre of the park and proceeded to torture a totally harassed Rangers back-line.  As the 'Bhoys' began to create more and more chances, only 'keeper Goram stood between them and a resounding victory.  If truth be known, the home side were never in it, although they might have reached the break still level but for a piece of magic from Collins.

Right on the stroke of half-time, Celts were awarded a free-kick just outside the box and the stage was set.  Just as he had done the previous season against Rangers at Ibrox (1-1, 30.4.94), John curled a glorious shot around the wall to score.  From virtually the same spot, he had produced virtually the same shot - only this time it was Goram who was left helpless as opposed to young reserve 'keeper Scott.

Barely two minutes into the second period, this well-deserved lead was doubled when a snap shot from Paul McStay (following the sweetest of Peter Grant passes) left the Scotland 'keeper helpless again.  Although there was no more scoring, the visitors were unlucky not to make it three when McStay's thunderous drive crashed off the post with Goram beaten.

So, 2-0 it was and both McStay and Collins had proved once again that, on their day, they were outstanding.  It must be said, though, that everybody played their part in what was a totally convincing triumph at the home of their greatest rivals.  Tommy Burns' first sojourn to Ibrox, as manager of Celtic, had proved more enjoyable than even he could have dared hope when the new season's fixture list had been published some weeks previously.

BURNS' BHOYS had indeed done him, themselves and the club proud.

BURNS' BHOYS

BURNS' BHOYS  BURNS' BHOYS

BURNS

# OLD FIRM QUIZ

1. Celtic were 1-0 down at half-time in the 1966 'Ne'erday' game. What was the final score?

2. Who scored for the 'Bhoys' in the 1-1 draw of late December 1999?

3. What was unique about the first four weeks of Season 1971-72?

4. Can you name the scorers when Celtic crushed Rangers 7-1 in the League Cup Final of October 1957?

5. Three players were sent off during a league encounter in October 1987. Who were they?

6. Jimmy Quinn entered the record books following the Scottish Cup Final defeat of Rangers in 1904. Why?

7. True or false - Lubomir Moravcik scored a hat-trick in the famous 5-1 league demolition of Rangers in November 1998.

8. Celtic and Rangers contested the Scottish Cup Final of 1969. What was the score?

9. What was the attendance for the Celtic/Rangers 'Centenary' Scottish Cup Final of May 1973?

10. Celtic lifted the league title by defeating Rangers in their last game of Season 1978/79. True or false?

Answers on page 64.

# HAIL THE CENTENARY DOUBLE!

## Scottish Cup Final, 14th May, 1988
## Celtic 2  Dundee United 1
## McAvennie (75, 89 mins)

Just as fifty years earlier, when Celtic had capped the club's Golden Jubilee year by clinching the commemorative Empire Exhibition Trophy outright, so the gods of football smiled on the 'Bhoys' in their Centenary Season of 1987/88.  The omens had certainly been good with the return of club legend Billy McNeill as manager (for the second time) but even with 'Caesar' back in charge, the possibility of a League and Cup Double seemed remote.  Current champions Rangers (with Graeme Souness at the helm) would be impossible to shift . . . so everybody said!

Once again, the outcome of the 'Old Firm' derbies would prove crucial in the title race.  Of the four league encounters that season, Celts won three and drew the other.  A 2-1 Ibrox triumph in late March had given the 'Bhoys' a six point cushion at the top and confirmed them as champions elect.  In fact, they had been in pole position since beating Hibernian 1-0 at Easter Road the previous November.

With Rangers having fallen by the wayside in the Scottish Cup (courtesy of Dunfermline), it was Dundee United who lined up to contest the final with Celtic on an unusually hot May day at Hampden. After a scoreless first-half, it was the Taysiders who struck early in the second period with Kevin Gallacher's blistering shot giving the 'Arab' travelling support plenty to celebrate. Celtic's double, fairytale dream seemed to be fading fast. Or was it?

Following the arrival of substitutes Billy Stark and Mark McGhee, the game turned in Celtic's favour. Then, with some fifteen minutes to go, Frank McAvennie headed home an Anton Rogan cross and extra-time beckoned. Amazingly, however, with virtually the last attack of the game, the blonde striker famously claimed his second of the half by firing home through a ruck of players (after a Joe Miller corner) and it was all over, bar the celebrations.

A glorious Centenary Double had been achieved, with a deserved place in Celtic's Hall of Fame for that day's team :

McKnight, Morris, Rogan, Aitken, McCarthy, Whyte, (Stark), Miller, McStay, McAvennie, Walker, (McGhee) and Burns .

# CELTIC IN EUROPE

1 Name the teams beaten on the road to European Cup glory in Season 1966/67.

2 Following this marvellous achievement, the 'Hoops' played the World Club Champions at Celtic Park in September 1967. Who were they?

3 He was the first Scot to score the winning goal in a European Cup Final. He was, of course?

4 The season Celtic lost in the final of the European Cup, the club did, in fact, win a European Trophy. What was it?

5 Name the so-called 'unbeatable' English premiership side who Celtic defeated in the European Cup semi-final of 1970.

6 As European Club Champions, Celts played Real Madrid in a Testimonial game for one of the latter's greatest-ever players. Name him.

7 Name the player who tore apart Red Star Belgrade in the famous 5-1 victory of Season 1968/69.

8 Do you know the famous story behind this Celt's amazing performance that night?

9 When Celtic played Benfica in the European Cup of 1969/70, the aggregate score was 3-3. How was the tie eventually settled?

10 Captain Billy McNeill scored a famous late, late winner against which side in the European Cup quarter-final of Season 1966/67.

Answers on page 64.

# A RARE

# LUBOMIR MORAVCIK

Sometimes during a football match, if you are really lucky, there is a moment that the mind captures and refuses to let go. In this particular case, it was not a goal (although four were scored that day) but one of those joyously impudent moments that are all too rare in today's modern game. Certainly the Celtic faithful, who had gathered to watch the 'home' league encounter with Hearts in late August 1999, were still talking about this one particular incident long after the final whistle had sounded. No prizes for guessing that the player involved was Lubo Moravcik.

Very few supporters had any knowledge of the player when it was confirmed that manager Josef Venglos was bringing the Slovak to Scotland to sign for the club in early November, 1998. Of course, that all changed rather quickly, after his stunning performance some three weeks later when Rangers were ripped to pieces in the 5-1 league demolition at Celtic Park. Apart from scoring two marvellous goals that day, Lubo's outfield play was simply awesome as the reigning league champions suffered their worst defeat in years.

Unfortunately, after picking up an injury against Motherwell in late February of Season 1998/99, the player missed most of the rest of the league campaign. There can be no doubt that his ceativity was sorely missed. Last year, however, it was a different story and Moravcik started thirty-eight games in total, a tally only equalled by defender Vidar Riseth. For good measure, he also claimed nine goals, including 'doubles' in the league clashes of December and May with Hibernian and Aberdeen respectively.

Although the player is now in the latter stages of his footballing life, the feeling persists that Season 2000/2001 could still be particularly special for both him and his club. The desire for success still burns within Moravcik who, surprisingly, does not have a winners' medal to his name, despite such an illustrious career. Not so long ago, remember, the star of EURO 2000, Zinedine Zidane, commented that Lubo could have held down his No.10 jersey at Juventus, such was his talent.

And a touch of that supreme talent was shown in the aforementioned league game with Hearts when, in the second period, he quite audaciously trapped and controlled the ball with . . . his backside! The Celtic fans just loved the sheer impudence of it all.

Just like they adore the player himself.

# CHALMERS

The Celtic scouting system and youth policy of the 1950s was a rich conveyor belt of talent which came to spectacular fruition with the hugely successful sides of the sixties and the seventies. In an era which pre-dated present day chequebook recruitment, the traditional tried and tested 'Cetic way' yielded many great and loyal club servants and none more so than Steve Chalmers, who joined the club from Ashfield Juniors in 1959.

Although never the most glamorous of players, Stevie was the sort of selfless, tireless front-runner who made others look good by creating space and chasing seemingly lost causes, turning them into goal chances for himself or a team-mate. He was the honest-to-goodness , industrious type which all great teams need and his huge Celtic heart inspired him to heights even he himself probably never imagined.

# HEART OF SOLID GREEN
## STEVE CHALMERS – A CELTIC LEGEND

His captain, Billy McNeill, maintained that, though quiet and unassuming, Chalmers had a hardness all of his own, a tenacity which unnerved opponents and epitomised the very heart and soul of the wonderful side he spearheaded – enthusiastic, tireless, fearless, dedicated, confident and, of course, skilful in the extreme.

In return, the often unsung hero was richly rewarded by periodic moments of high drama and sweet success. On two separate occasions, Stevie netted five goals at the quarter-final stage of the League Cup - firstly, in a second-leg six-goal romp against East Fife in 1964/65 and again, four seasons later, in the 10-0 demolition of Hamilton. The first of those blitzes earned him the temporary nickname 'Di Steviano', after the inimitable Real Madrid maestro Alfredo Di Stefano. The second, quite amazingly, was matched by Bobby Lennox's own five in the same game.

On a somewhat higher level, Chalmers put the icing on the cake of the joyous 4-0 hiding of Rangers in the 1969 Scottish Cup Final, with a memorable fourth goal, jauntily stuck past 'keeper Martin and central defender McKinnon as they both converged on him following his long, angled run-in from the left. It was Stevie, too, who broke the agonising tension of the 1967 European Cup quarter-final, second leg against Vojvodina with the crucial opening strike to level the tie at Celtic Park . . . and the ultimate accolade followed with his decisive touch for the historic Lisbon winner itself. How fitting that one of Celtic's humblest, most loyal and most likeable characters should savour that supreme moment.

When Stevie left to join Morton at the end of season 1970/71, following the last-ever competitive appearance of the Lisbon Lions (a 6-1 defeat of Clyde in the final league match of another Championship year), he did so as second only to the incomparable Jimmy McGrory in the Celtic all-time scoring charts to that point.

Enough said.

# FIND THE CELT

## The names of 10 Celtic Legends are hidden somewhere in this letter puzzle.

### Can you find them?

```
W E C J S H L V P R N L Y Z O D T Q X H
L K J H G F M C G R O R Y I U T D P W A
N O U A Q R T J O G L J G D T Z X V B N
I E X Y L S N R U B K J H G F U Y T R E
E I U T N E R T U D G J L C V N G I P V
T N M N B I C H G K O I U I Y R E K A A
S R D E L A N E Y L K J H G F D T I O N
A E K J B V F C D N E K T I A Y T E C S
P F S N I L L O C D L U A J H G F O T W
P O I J H G T F R D E S W Z Q U N J H Z
```

# PICK OF THE TROPHY ROOMS (1)

## THE GLASGOW EXHIBITION CUP (1902)

This spectacular silver trophy was originally the property of Rangers Football Club, who had won it following an eight-club Scottish competition to mark the Glasgow International Tournament of 1901.  A bruising, controversial final against Celtic had resulted in a 3-1 victory for the Govan team and the presentation of this magnificent example of the silversmith's art.

The following year, the 'Old Firm' came together again in a foursome with Everton and Sunderland (the English Champions and runners-up) to play a mini-tournament in support of the victims of the tragic Ibrox disaster of April 1902 - twenty six people had been killed and nearly six hundred injured when a terracing collapsed during the Scotland/England international.  The competition was inevitably elevated into a sort of British Championship by the press of the day and Rangers saw fit to raise the stakes and reflect the hyped-up status of the event by offering their Exhibition Cup as a permanent prize.

It just had to be a Celtic/Rangers final and so it proved, as Celtic disposed of Sunderland, while Rangers knocked out Everton, leaving the Glasgow rivals to re-contest the trophy they had so recently disputed.  Following a 1-1 draw in the first game, the 'Hoops' eventually triumphed 3-2 after extra-time in the replay.  And that is the reason why a trophy inscribed 'Won by Rangers FC' now has a permanent place inside Celtic Park!

Footnote : Celtic enjoyed a much more emphatic victory over the 'Light Blues' some weeks later in another match in aid of the Disaster Fund.  There was no trophy on that occasion, with only prestige (and medals sponsored by Bovril) being at stake as Celtic thumped their great rivals 7-2, helped by a 'hat-trick' from Jimmy Quinn.

# PICK OF THE TROPHY ROOMS (2)

## THE CORONATION CUP (1953)

Celtic FC has a proud tradition of success in special 'one-off' competitions in which the prize becomes the outright property of the winner. No matter the team's form, such special circumstances seem to bring out the best in the club, as the Coronation Cup of 1953 bears witness.

The competition featured the top clubs of the time from both Scotland and England : Arsenal, Manchester United, Tottenham Hotspur, Newcastle United, Celtic, Rangers, Hibernian and Aberdeen. To be honest, Celtic's inclusion was probably more a reflection of the team's reputation and crowd-pulling potential than its standing at the time. Nonetheless, the unlikely events of that summer were destined to weave their way into Celtic folklore and become immortalised in one of the more imaginative club anthems.

When battle commenced, the 'Bhoys' surprised everyone by beating the English Champions Arsenal 1-0. As if that wasn't enough, they went on to dispose of Manchester United (first-round conquerors of Rangers) 2-1 and set up an unlikely all-Scottish final against Hibernian who had beaten both Spurs and Newcastle. So it was that all roads led to Hampden on 30th May, 1953 and the old stadium was transformed into a veritable sea of green!

Celtic took the lead in twenty-eight minutes, courtesy of a typically thunderous long-range Neil Mochan shot which had been set up by the great Willie Fernie. Although Hibs stormed the Celtic goal in the second-half, the defence stood firm with Jock Stein (the man himself!), Bobby Evans and 'keeper Johnny Bonnar, in particular, truly outstanding. Three minutes from time, an Evans interception and pass sparked the move which ended in a second, decisive strike by Walsh.

Another memorable chapter had been written in the magical history of The Celtic Football Club!

Team : Bonnar, Haughney, Rollo, Evans, Stein, McPhail, Collins, Walsh, Mochan, Peacock and Fernie.

# celtic
## the honours

### League Championships (36 in total)

1892/93, 1893/94, 1895/96, 1897/98, 1904/05, 1905/06, 1906/07, 1907/08, 1908/09, 1909/10, 1913/14, 1914/15, 1915/16, 1916/17, 1918/19, 1921/22, 1925/26, 1935/36, 1937/38, 1953/54, 1965/66, 1966/67, 1967/68, 1968/69, 1969/70, 1970/71, 1971/72, 1972/73, 1973/74, 1976/77, 1978/79, 1980/81, 1981/82, 1985/86, 1987/88, 1997/98.

### Scottish Cups (30)

1892, 1899, 1900, 1904, 1907, 1908, 1911, 1912, 1914, 1923, 1925, 1927, 1931, 1933, 1937, 1951, 1954, 1965, 1967, 1969, 1971, 1972, 1974, 1975, 1977, 1980, 1985, 1988, 1989, 1995.

### Scottish League Cups (11)

1956, 1957, 1965, 1966, 1967, 1968, 1969, 1974, 1982, 1997, 2000.

### SPECIALS

Glasgow Exhibition Cup (1902)

Scottish League Commemorative Shield (1904/05 - 1909/10)

Empire Exhibition Trophy (1938)

Victory in Europe Cup (1945)

St. Mungo Cup (1951)

Coronation Cup (1953)

European Champions' Cup (1967)

# jonathan gould

First appearance for Celtic was in 'Coca-Cola' Cup, second round tie against Berwick Rangers in August 1997. From then until that famous last game of the season against St. Johnstone, he never missed a game, conceding only twenty-two League Championship goals on the road to glory. Was one of only four Celts who appeared in more than forty games for the club throughout Season 1998/99. In another life, he was in goal for Coventry when they thrashed Liverpool (whose line-up on the day included a certain John Barnes) 5-1.

# tom Boyd

Just like Chris Sutton several years later, Tom Boyd arrived at Celtic Park from Chelsea. The full-back has been club captain since Paul McStay's playing career came to an end and the midfielder announced his retirement in May 1997. Since then, Boyd has lifted silverware on three separate occasions, leading his team to the 'double' of League Championship and League Cup in Season 1997/98 and the League Cup triumph over Aberdeen in March 2000. Solid and reliable.

# jackie mcnamara

Named 'Player of the Year' by his fellow professionals for Season 1997/98. This followed his 'Young Player' trophy, two years earlier. Survived a career-threatening injury back in March 1989 when, during a training session, his right leg was shattered in two places. Appeared thirty-one times for the 'Hoops' throughout Season 1999/2000. Quiet superb going forward.

# johan mjallby

An intimidating presence at the heart of the Celtic rearguard, Johan netted four times in Season 1999/2000 - against St. Johnstone (3-0, 7.8.99), Cwmbran Town (4-0, EUFA Cup 26.8.99), Ayr (4-0,13.1.99) and Dundee (3-0, 12.2.2000). Won a Championship medal with AIK Stockholm before heading south to Glasgow in November 1998. Stalwart of the Swedish national side (along with Henrik Larsson), Johan scored for his country during EURO 2000. Also claimed a famous winner for Sweden when they defeated England 2-1 in a qualifying game for the same tournament back in September 1998.

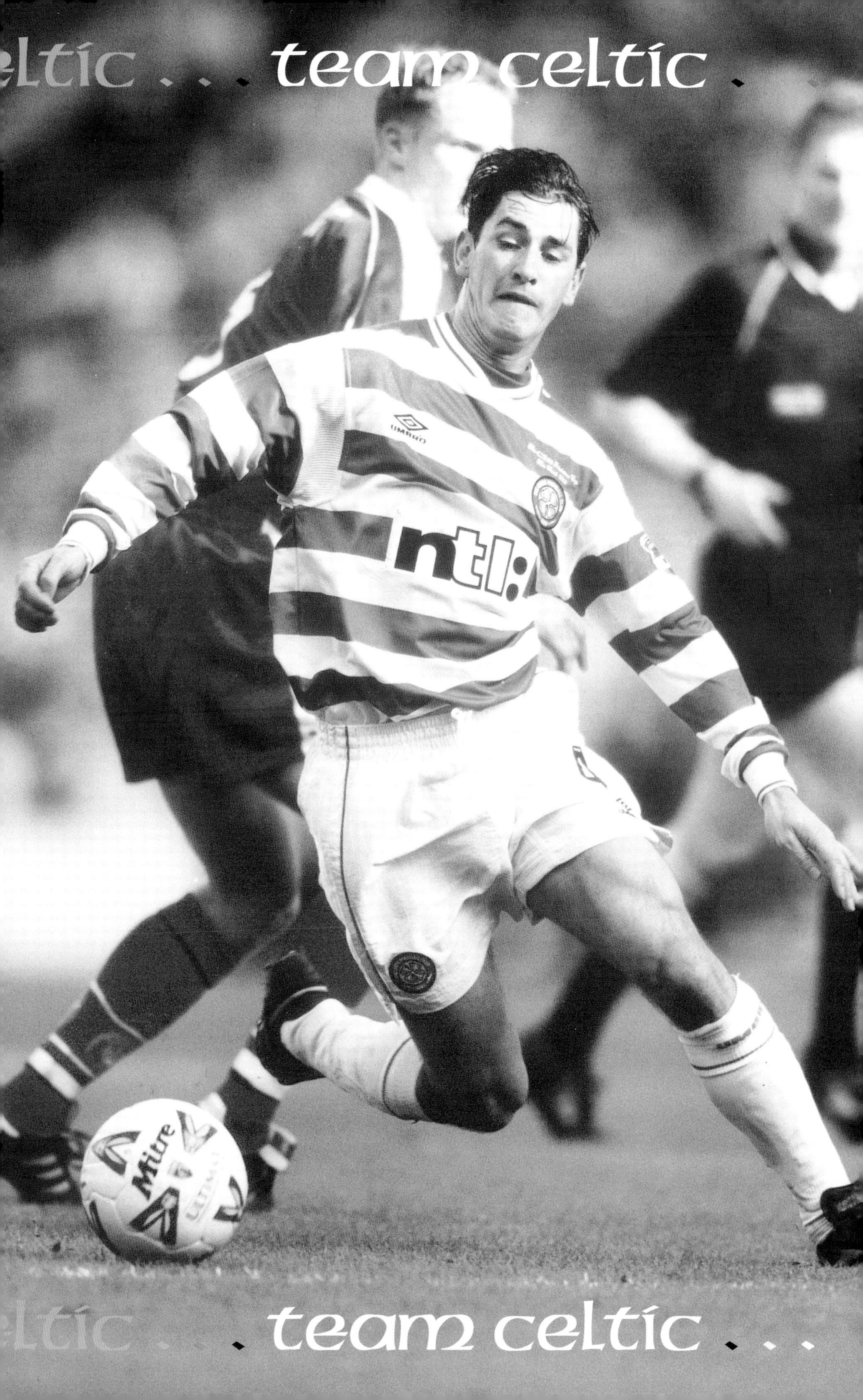
UMBRO
ntl:
Mitre

## alan stubbs

Appeared thirty-two times 'at the back' for Celtic in Season 1999/2000 and was, on each and every occasion, solid as a rock. Silenced the Ibrox crowd in January 1999 when he curled the ball home for his side's first in the 2-2 draw. Nearly doubled his tally in the same game but his header rebounded off the bar with 'keeper Klos well beaten. If only. . . .

## olivier tebily

Having arrived from Sheffield United at the start of last season, the French defender made twenty-eight first-team appearances throughout the various campaigns. A solitary goal was claimed in the EUFA Cup game with Cwmbran Town. A cult favourite with the Celtic masses.

## stephane mahe

The accomplished and stylish left full-back scored four times last year - in the games with Dundee (2-1, 21.8.99), Aberdeen (6-0, 11.12.99), Dundee (2-2, 15.4.2000) and Hibernian (1-1, 22.4.2000). Stephane played against Celtic in the Cup Winners' Cup Tournament of Season 1995/96 when he was with Paris St. Germain. Plays with a passion for the jersey.

## vidar riseth

No player made more appearances than the big Norwegian last season. His total of thirty-eight (in all tournaments) was only equalled by Lubo Moravcik. Managed to find the net on only one occasion but it was a rather special occasion! Vidar, of course, scored the opener when Celtic lifted the CIS Insurance/League Cup in March after beating Aberdeen 2-0 at Hampden. Was part of the Norwegian squad for EURO 2000 in Holland and Belgium last summer but only appeared for a short period as a substitute late on in one of the games.

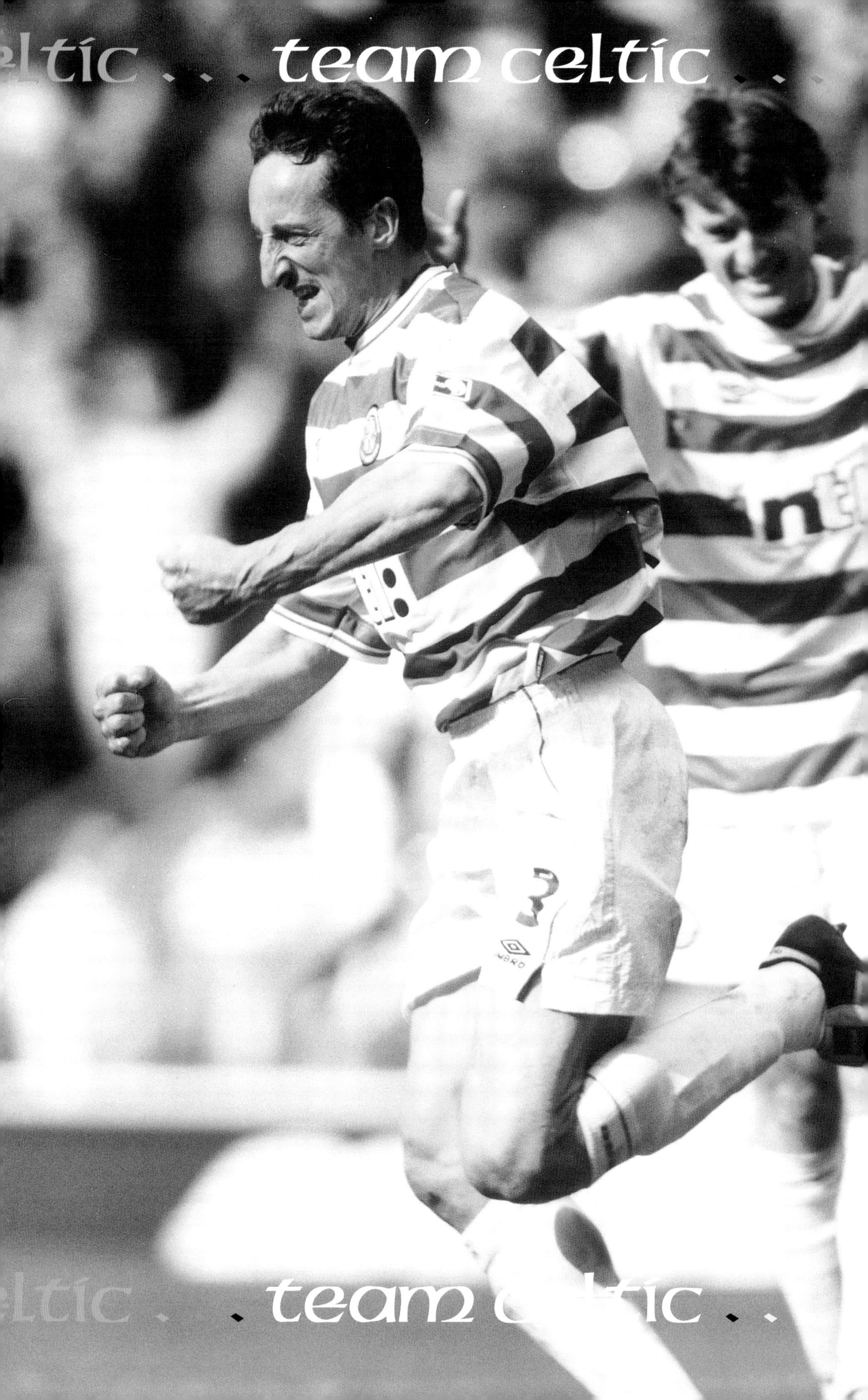

# paul lambert

Proud owner of a European Cup Winner's medal (following Borussia Dortmund's 1997 win over Juventus), Paul Lambert also won a Scottish Cup Medal with St. Mirren back in 1987.  Surprisingly, netted only once last season when Aberdeen were crushed 6-0 in mid December.  Everybody still remembers his thunderous shot in the 'Old Firm' Scottish Cup Final of 1999 that left Rangers 'keeper Klos rooted to the spot. An inch lower and Celtic would have been ahead!  Without a question of doubt, midfielder Paul Lambert is one of Celtic's best signings over the last few years.

# morten wieghorst

Injury clouded the Danish midfielder's season in 1999/2000.  Made sixteen starts and netted, for good measure, four times in games with St. Johnstone (both league encounters of 7.8.99 and 24.10.99 - when he scored the last-minute winner in a 2-1 victory), Dundee (1-0, 1.12.99) and Hibernian (4-0, 4.12.99).  Always gives 100%, regardless of the circumstances.

# lubomír moravcík

Brought to the club by Josef Venglos, Lubo first appeared in the green of Celtic when Dundee were demolished 6-1 in November 1998.  Two weeks later, he was an absolute revelation, scoring twice as the Rangers rearguard chased his shadow in that famous 5-1 rout of the Govan side.  Along with Vidar Riseth, he appeared more times than any other player in Season 1999/2000.  Lubo's nine goals (in thirty-eight outings) included 'doubles' in games with Hibernian (4-0, 4.12.99) and Aberdeen (5-1, 6.5.99) and single strikes against Hearts (2-1, 20.11.99), Aberdeen (6-0, 11.12.99), Dundee United (4-1, 18.12.99), and Hearts (2-3, 5.2.2000).  His other strike was, of course, the winner in the League Cup semi-final victory over Kilmarnock in mid February.

# eyal berkovic

Appeared thirty times for the 'Hoops' in Season 1999/2000, scoring ten goals in the process.  His tally comprised 'doubles' in the games with Hearts (4-0, 29.8.99) and Rangers (2-4, 7.11.99) as well as single strikes in the encounters with Cwmbran Town (6-0, EUFA Cup 12.8.99), Dundee United (1-2, 15.8.99), Aberdeen (7-0, 16.10.99), Motherwell (2-3, 27.11.99), Kilmarnock (4-2, 2.4.2000) and Motherwell (4-0, 5.4.2000). 'Player of the Year' for Season 2000/2001 in Scotland?  Any bets?

# stilian petrov

Began to show his undoubted (real) form towards the latter part of last season with a series of powerhouse midfield performances for the team. The young Bulgarian even made the scoresheet when Dundee were soundly thrashed 6-2 in the early March 2000 'home' game at Celtic Park. At the ripe old age of 21(!), Stilian is already a regular in the national side, which is hardly surprising as the youngster is reported to be the best midfielder for his age group in Eastern Europe. Naturally a player who can only improve with time.

# chris sutton

Filled both the centre-half and centre-forward positions with Norwich before going on to form the famous 'SAS' partnership with Alan Shearer at Blackburn Rovers. A striker of the highest quality, Chris Sutton led the English Premiership scoring charts some three years ago with eighteen goals in one season for Blackburn. Chelsea manager Gianluca Vialli then paid £10 million to take the player south to the London club but this move, surprisingly, never quite worked out for the player. And so it came to pass that, at the start of Season 2000/2001, Chris arrived in Glasgow to join Celtic for a fee of £6 million. Martin O'Neill's first signing had just broken the Scottish transfer record, established when Eyal Berkovic moved from West Ham to our fair city the previous year.

# tommy johnson

One of the genuine joys of the latter part of Season 1999/2000 was the return to full fitness of striker Tommy Johnson. Obviously the highlight of this period was his goal in the CIS Insurance/League Cup Final against Aberdeen at Hampden (2-0, 19.3.2000) but it is also worth recalling the player's two 'hat-tricks' against Dundee (6-2, 1.3.2000) and Aberdeen (5-1, 6.5.2000) as well as his 'double' in the 4-0 defeat of Motherwell in early April. The player claimed a total of ten goals in only eight starting appearances for Celtic from March through to the end of the season. Not a bad average!

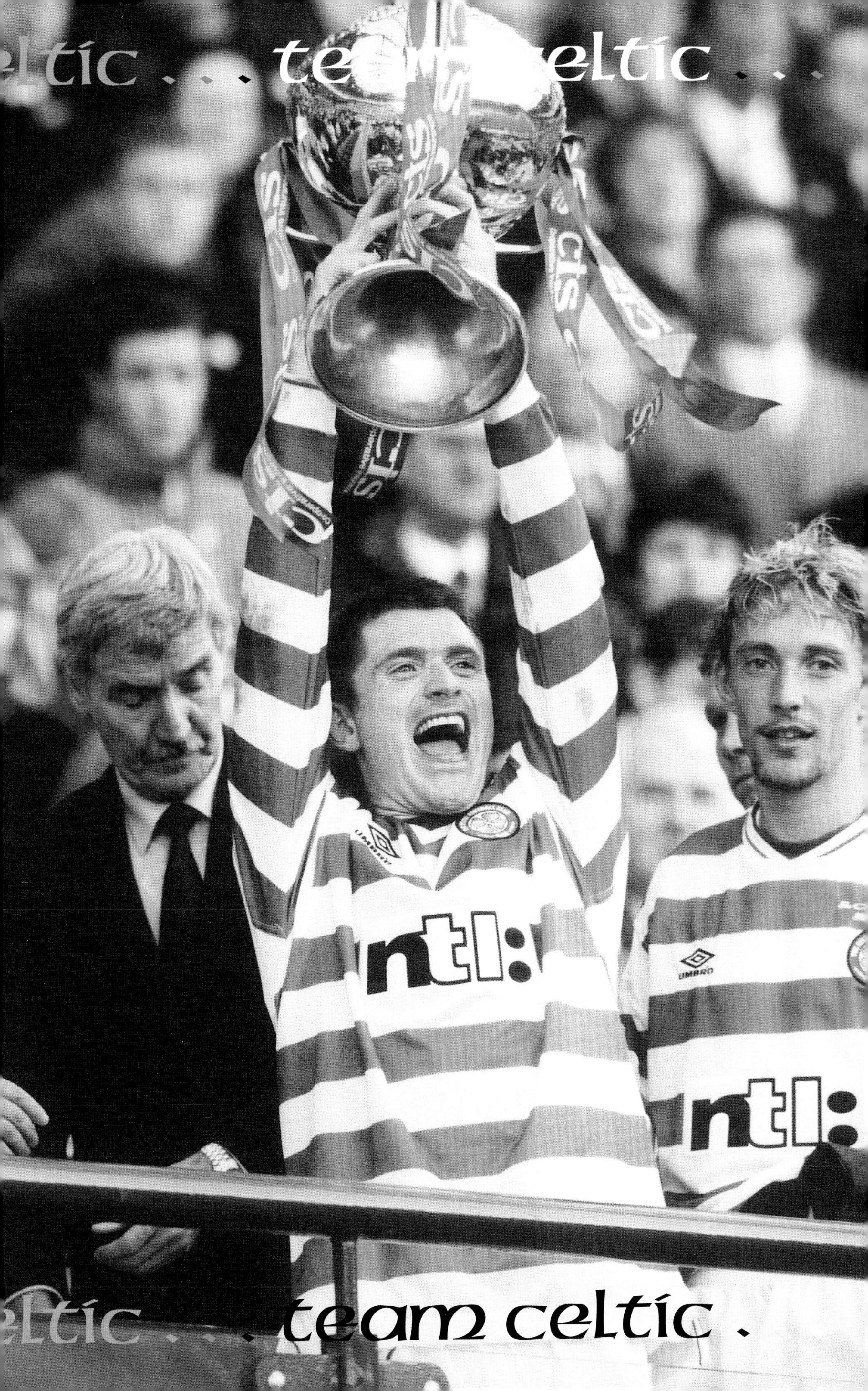

eltic . . . team celtic . . .
cis
ntl:
UMBRO
ntl:
eltic . . . team celtic .

## mark Burchill

It's sometimes easy to forget that Burchill is still a youngster in terms of both playing career and age.  Last year, he netted nine times in sixteen starts as well as claiming three additional goals after appearing as a substitute during matches.  The pick of the bunch were, no doubt, his winners at Kilmarnock (1-0, 12.9.99) and, against Dundee United, at Tannadice (1-0, 2.5.2000) as well as a 'double' in the game with St. Johnstone (4-1, 11.3.2000).  For sure, the arrival of Chris Sutton will  bring out the best in the player as he 'fights' for one of those striking positions in the team.  Scored both Celtic goals in the pre-season friendly with FC Copenhagen in Denmark , July 2000.

## henrik Larsson

Sorely missed throughout last season following that dreadful injury in Lyon whilst on EUFA Cup duty with Celtic.  Any team would miss such a charismatic player who, the previous year remember, had been voted not only Scotland's 'Player of the Year' but also Sweden's 'Footballer of the Year'.  Thankfully he fully recovered from that career-threatening double leg break and was playing again for his beloved 'Hoops' by the end of the league campaign.  Anyone who saw his most impressive performances for Sweden throughout EURO 2000 in Holland and Belgium will testify that the 'old' Henrik Larsson is alive and well! And for that, we should all be thankful.

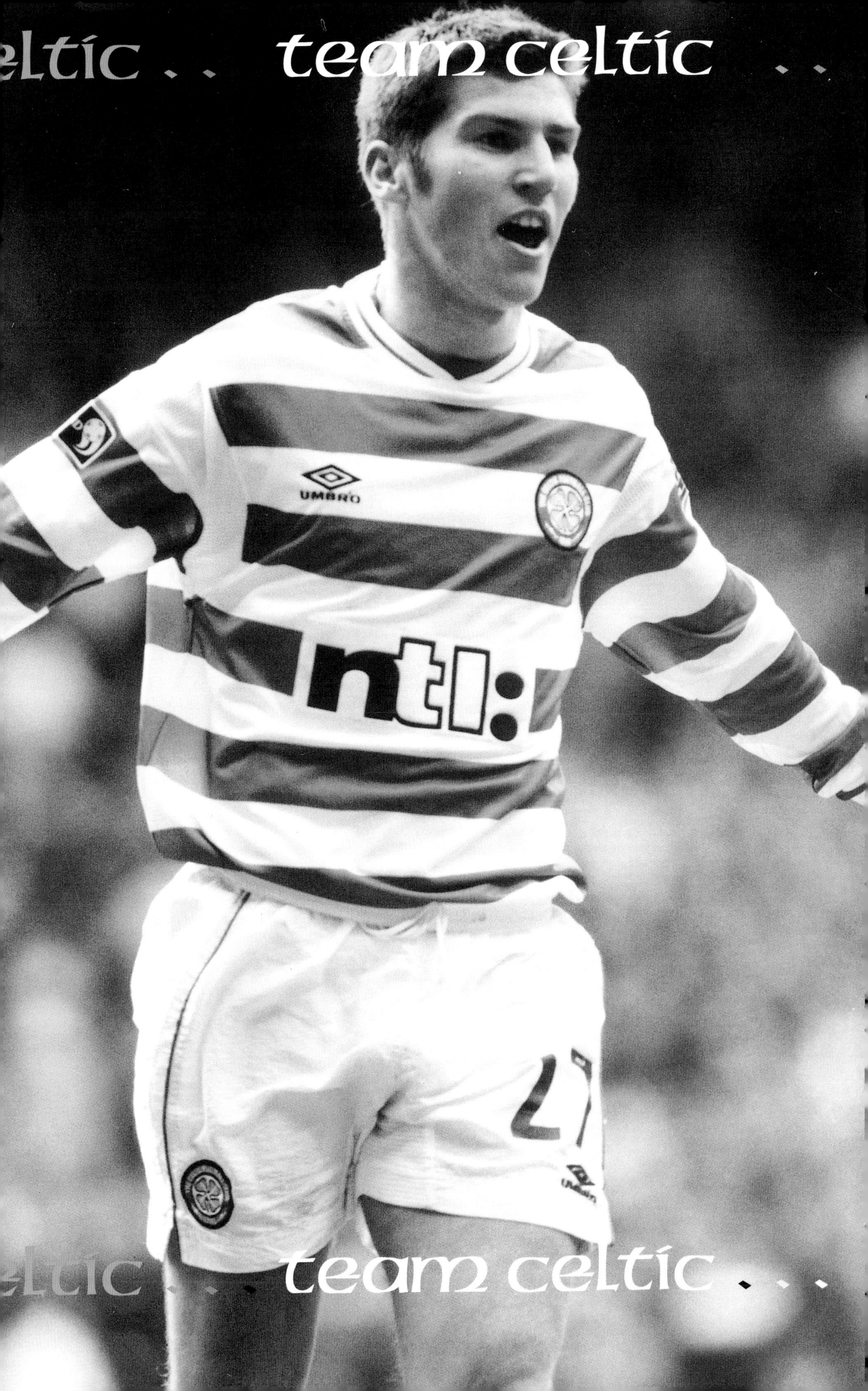

team celtic . . .
UMBRO
ntl:
team celtic . . .

# CELTIC
# CUP QUIZ

1   Who scored for the 'Bhoys' when the team lifted the CIS Insurance League Cup in March 2000?

2   In the same game, whose audacious 30 yard lob crashed off the bar with Aberdeen 'keeper Leighton helpless?

3   Name Celtic's opponents in the 1953 Coronation Cup Final after Manchester United, Arsenal and Rangers had all fallen by the wayside.

4   What was the result and who scored?

5   In the club's Centenary Season of 1987/88, Celtic defeated Dundee United 1-0 in the Scottish Cup Final with Frank McAvennie scoring the winner.  True or false?

6   Name the English Premiership side that Celtic beat to lift the 1938 Empire Exhibition Trophy

7   When did Celtic last win the Scottish Cup?

8   Captain __ lifted the trophy that day following the only goal of the game scored by __.  Fill in the missing names.

9   Tommy Burns won only one trophy as manager of Celtic. What was it?

10  Name the legendary manager during whose stewardship Celtic won an astonishing 59 Cup competitions?

Answers on page 64.

### Season 1965/66

Celtic's first Championship in 12 years (by two points from Rangers) was secured on the last day of the campaign with a 1-0 win over Motherwell at Fir Park.  Joe McBride was top scorer with 31 as the team netted 106 goals in 34 league games.  Result of the season was, undoubtably, the 'Ne'erday' triumph over Rangers when the 'Bhoys', after being one down at the interval, staged a magnificent second-half comeback to secure a famous 5-1 victory.  Lost to Liverpool in the semi-final of the European Cup Winners' Cup after a superb last-minute 'winning' Bobby Lennox goal was, many thought, wrongly judged as 'offside'.  The League Cup also returned to Celtic Park, for the first time since 1957.

### Season 1966/67

The greatest of all seasons included not only the League Championship, Scottish Cup and League Cup but also, of course, the European Cup.  At home, the team scored an astonishing 111 goals in 34 league encounters (average 3.26 per game!) and, in Europe, netted 16 times before Tommy Gemmell and Steve Chalmers claimed the most famous two goals in Celtic's history in Lisbon's Estadio Nacional Stadium on the 25th May, 1967.

### Season 1967/68

Celtic lost just once in the League Championship campaign (1-0 to Rangers in only the second game of the season) and took the title by two points from their greatest rivals.  'Buzz Bomb' Bobby Lennox was top scorer with a tally of 32 strikes.  Both the League Cup and the Glasgow Cup were also retained.

### Season 1968/69

With Celtic again firing on all fronts, it was yet another clean sweep of domestic honours.  Rangers were crushed 4-0 in the Scottish Cup Final with goals from Billy McNeill (in just two minutes), Bobby Lennox, George Connelly and Steve Chalmers securing another famous victory over their oldest rivals.  Earlier on in the season, Hibs had been swept away 6-2 in the League Cup Final.  Away from Scottish action, one of the truly great nights at Celtic Park saw Red Star Belgrade beaten 5-1, with winger Jimmy Johnstone virtually destroying the proud European outfit almost single-handedly.  Reached the quarter-final of the European Cup.

**IN A**

### Season 1969/70

Champions again (Rangers languished twelve points adrift in second place), this Celtic side came so, so close to European Cup glory. After disposing of English Champions Leeds United in the two-leg, semi-final (with victories both 'away' at Elland Road and 'home' at Hampden Park - in front of more than 134,000!), they lost narrowly to the Dutch of Feyenoord in the final, eventually going down 2-1 after extra-time. Both the League Cup and the Glasgow Cup joined the League Trophy in the east end of the city.

### Season 1970/71

'6 In A Row' was achieved by two points from Aberdeen, with Rangers not even finishing in the first three places of the Championship race. For the seventh time in the club's history, the 'double' of League and Scottish Cup was won.

### Season 1971/72

Another marvellous Celtic campaign, with their 'red' rivals from the north of Scotland again finishing in second place but this time ten points off the winning total of sixty. The season ended with one of those memorable 'Celtic' Scottish Cup Finals - opponents Hibernian had six goals (including a 'Dixie' Deans 'hat-trick') blasted past them on a day when the 'Bhoys' were really quite magnificent. A penalty shoot-out was lost to Inter Milan in the semi-final of the European Cup, thus denying Celtic a third appearance in the final of this most prestigious of tournaments.

### Season 1972/73

Although they lost in both the finals of the League Cup and Scottish cup, Celtic's 14 match unbeaten run (from February) in the title race ensured a one point Championship victory over the other half of the 'Old Firm'.

# ROW

### Season 1973/74

It was another 'double' year for Celts as the Scottish Cup returned to the trophy rooms following a comprehensive 3-0 triumph over Dundee United in the final. This time it was Hibernian who ran the 'Bhoys' close in the Championship, finally taking the runner-up prize four points behind the winning total of fifty-three. Amazingly, this ninth Championship in succession was clinched, like all the others, away from Celtic Park! In Europe, the team reached the semi-final stage before losing out to the cynicism of Spain's Atletico Madrid.

It was indeed the best of times. But it should never be forgotten that, sooner or later, the good times always return.

# CELTIC
## LEAGUE
## CHAMPIONSHIP
# QUIZ

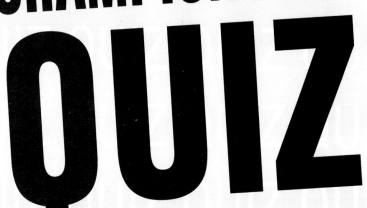

1. Who scored for Celtic when Dundee United were beaten 2-0 on the last day of Season 1999/2000?

2. Henrik Larsson was top scorer in Season 1997/98 when the 'Bhoys' lifted the League title. True or false?

3. Name the striker who claimed a 'hat-trick' on the night that Dundee were crushed 6-2 at Celtic Park in early March 2000.

4. Apart from Henrik Larsson, identify the other two Celts who reached double figures in the league scoring charts for the Championship Season of 1997/98.

5. In goal-scoring terms, what was unique about the trio of Championship Seasons 1965/66, 1966/67 and 1967/68?

6. On the last day of Season 1982/83 at Ibrox, Celtic were 2-0 down at half-time. What was the final score?

7. In Championship Season 1997/98, Celtic conceded fewer goals than any other team. How few?

8. With the score tied at 1-1, whose powerful header hit the bar during last season's late December 1999 clash with Rangers?

9. How many goals did Aberdeen concede to Celtic in their first three encounters last season?

10. How many League Championships have Celtic won over the years?

Answers on page 64.

# FAMOUS VICTORY

## THE GREATEST OF ALL TRIUMPHS OVER RANGERS
### League Cup Final, 19th October, 1957

### Celtic 7    Rangers 1

This was the very first 'Old Firm' League Cup Final. Most neutrals felt that Rangers, league champions for the last two seasons, were clear favourites to lift the trophy even although Celtic had captured this particular piece of silverware the previous year, finally defeating Partick Thistle 3-0 at the second attempt, after a goalless draw. (It had been the 'Bhoys' first-ever triumph in the competition since its inception for Season 1946/47). As per usual, an intriguing confrontation was anticipated between the two great Glasgow rivals but, in truth, few of the 82,000 spectators could have dreamt of the massacre that was about to follow!

Right from the start, Celtic were in command, with the midfield trio of Willie Fernie, Bobby Evans and Bertie Peacock controlling the game. Sammy Wilson's volley opened the scoring before both Bobby Collins and Charlie Tully were foiled by the crossbar and post respectively. Just before the break, Neil Mochan deservedly made it two and everybody took a breather.

If Rangers thought that the second period would bring a welcome change of fortune, they were wrong. Very wrong! As Celts swarmed all over them right from kick-off, it just got worse (or better, depending upon your point of view!) and the 'Light Blues' were swept away in a green tidal wave. Another five goals followed - comprising a wonderful threesome from Billy McPhail, a second from Mochan for his 'double' and, the icing on the cake, a Willie Fernie penalty near the end of the ninety minutes. The rout was complete and the most glorious of all 'Old Firm' victories had been achieved the traditional 'Celtic' way. That is with skill, skill . . . and more skill!

This record result for a Scottish national cup final has become, understandably, a major part of the club's folklore. Not as prestigious as the historic European Cup win of 25th May 1967 but, in the eyes of many fans, just as important.

The Celtic heroes that autumn day were :
Beattie, Donnelly, Fallon, Fernie, Evans, Peacock, Tully, Collins, McPhail, Wilson and Mochan.

# CELTIC LEGENDS
# QUIZ

1 Nicknamed 'The Quiet Assassin'. Name this famous midfielder from the early 1970s.

2 In 1956, he became the first Celtic captain to lift the Scottish League Cup. A truly inspirational player.

3 Scored the opener on that famous day in Lisbon. 'Big Tam' was also the spot-kick expert with 31 goals in 34 attempts during his time in the 'Hoops'.

4 One of the great 'keepers, he gained his first international cap at the ripe old age of 36, making him Scotland's oldest-ever international debutant.

5 Goal-scorer supreme, he had netted an astonishing 37 goals before Christmas in the 'Season in the Sun' of 1966/67.

6 His winning header in the 1965 Scottish Cup Final was the real beginning of the Jock Stein era.

7 In Season 1998/99, he netted an amazing 38 goals in 48 games . . . and now he's back!

8 Club captain when Celtic won the 'double' in their Centenary season.

9 Nicknamed the 'Pocket Dynamo'in the 1950s, he was an influential member of the side that crushed Rangers 7-1 in the League Cup Final of 1957.

10 Scored a 'hat-trick' when Celtic demolished Hibs 6-1 in the Scottish Cup Final of 1972.

Answers on page 64.

# FIND THE CELT

The names of 10 current Celtic personalities
(although not all players!)
are hidden somewhere in this letter puzzle.

## Can you find them?

```
D N B V C X L A R S S O N K J H G F D N
Y O U Y T R E W Q S D F G H J K L N O I
O F G H J K L M N U T Y O P L S E H A M
B F W O N E I L L Z P H F L A M B E R T
M N H Y T R F Y P D S T U B B S N M L U
A S T F G H J K L M N H T E S I R E H G
P L O K O J M N H Y G H T L R D S E O J
Z X C V U N M K J H O U V O R T E P L T
U P K J L P K N B F R S X U Y T D G K L
A S D F D H J K L P O N O T T U S B N M
```

Answers on page 64.

# answers

## olɒ fiʀm quiz

1. 5-1 to Celtic.  2. Mark Viduka.
3. Celtic had already beaten Rangers three times - twice in the League
Cup (2-0, 3-0) and once in the league (3-2).  4. McPhail (3), Mochan (2), Fernie and Wilson.
5. Woods and Butcher of Rangers and McAvennie of Celtic.
6. He was the first Celt to score a hat-trick in the Scottish Cup Final.
7. False.  He only scored twice!  8. 4-0 for Celtic.  9. Approx. 122,700.
10. True.  They won 4-2 with 10 men (Doyle had been dismissed early in
the second half) after trailing 1-0 at the interval.

## celtic in euʀope quiz

1. FC Zurich, Nantes, Vojvodina, Dukla Prague and, finally, Inter Milan.  2. Penarol of Uruguay.
3. Steve Chalmers.  4. The prestigious French football newspaper 'France Football' named
Celtic as 'European Team of the Year'.  5. Leeds United.  6. Alfredo di Stefano.
7. Jimmy Johnstone.  8  Because of the player's fear of flying, manager Jock Stein promised
not to take him on the 'away' trip if a four goal lead was secured in the first-leg in Glasgow.
9. Celtic progressed on the toss of a coin.  Penalty shoot-outs had not yet been introduced
in the competition!  10. Vojvodina of Yugoslavia.

## celtic cup quiz

1. Vidar Riseth and Tommy Johnson.  2. Lubo Moravcik.  3. Hibs.  4. 2-0 for Celtic with Mochan and Walsh scoring.
5. False.  It was a 2-1 victory with 'Macca' claiming both.  6. Everton.  7. 27 May, 1995.
8. Paul McStay and Pierre Van Hooijdonk. 9. The aforementioned Scottish Cup of 1995.  10. Willie Maley.

## celtic league championship quiz

1. Simon Lynch and Mark Burchill.  2. True - with 19 goals in all tournaments.  3. Tommy Johnson.
4. Craig Burley and Simon Donnelly with 10 each.  5. Celtic netted over 100 league goals
each season - 106, 111 and 106 respectively.  6. 4-2 to Celtic.  7. Only 24 goals in 36 games.
8. Johan Mlallby's.  9. An astonishing 18!  10. 36 in total.

## celtic legenɒs quiz

1. David Hay.  2. Bobby Evans.  3. Tommy Gemmell.  4. Ronnie Simpson.  5. Joe McBride.
6. Billy McNeill.  7. Henrik Larsson.  8. Roy Aitken.  9. Bobby Collins.  10. 'Dixie' Deans.

## woʀɒseaʀch puzzle (1)

```
W E C J S H L V P R N L Y Z O D T Q X H
L K J N G F M C G R O R Y I U T D P W A
N O U A Q R T J O G L J G D T Z X V B N
I E X Y L S N R U B K J H G F U Y T R E
E I U T N E R T U D G J L C V N G I P V
T N M N B I C H G K O I U I Y R E K A A
S R D E L A N E Y L K J H G F D T I O N
A E K J B V F C D N E K T I A Y T E C S
P F S N I L L O C D L U A J H G F O T W
P O I J H G T F R D E S W Z Q U N J H Z
```

## woʀɒseaʀch puzzle (2)

```
D N B V C X L A R S S O N K J H G F D N
Y O U Y T R E W Q S D F G H J K L N O I
O F G H J K L M N U T Y O P L S E H A M
B F W O N E I L L Z P H F L A M B E R T
M N H Y T R F Y P D S T U B B S N M L U
A S T F G H J K L M N H T E S I R E H G
P L O K O J M N H Y G H T L R D S E O J
Z X C V U N M K J H O U V O R T E P L T
U P K J L P K N B F R S X U Y T D G K L
A S D F D H J K L P O N O T T U S B N M
```